D0321389

FARES, PLEASE!

·The Story of· Public Transport

STAN YORKE

COUNTRYSIDE BOOKS
NEWBURY BERKSHIRE

First published 2010
© Stan Yorke 2010

All rights reserved. No reproduction
permitted without the prior permission
of the publisher:

COUNTRYSIDE BOOKS
3 Catherine Road
Newbury, Berkshire

To view our complete range of books,
please visit us at
wwwcountrysidebooks.co.uk

ISBN 978 1 84674 199 9

Picture of the 'clippie' on the front cover
is courtesy of the London Transport Museum

Designed by Peter Davies, Nautilus Design
Produced through MRM Associates Ltd., Reading

Printed by Information Press, Oxford

CONTENTS

Introduction

Today the idea of 'public transport' possibly spans the widest cross-section of lives ever. To some it means a first class seat and cooked breakfast whilst cruising along at 80 or 90 mph towards the city on a relatively quiet and comfortable train. At the other end of the spectrum it is queuing for the seemingly always late bus and standing for the eternal start-stop ride to work. In between we have retired aunts jauntily riding a single deck bus from their village to the local town for a spot of shopping and coffee with a friend.

Yet the journey from the time when there was simply no public transport at all, to today is a ride through invention, politics and social upheaval. In this little book I strive to relive the moments of ingenuity, of Victorian splendour and sad demise.

I have been constantly surprised by just how long ago the various technical innovations were made. Often these ideas were shown to work but were simply too difficult to mass produce or more often were simply too heavy for the appalling roads of the time. Horse-drawn buses plied the London streets before Victoria came to the throne, as did early steam-driven versions. The railways started a revolution in longer distance transport which was well established throughout the land by the 1850s. The same decade saw the first horse-drawn trams at work.

When electricity and the petrol engine arrived the transport industry adopted these new ideas immediately, so much so that by 1914 the last horse-drawn bus had vanished from the London streets.

Intended to be more an introduction rather than a deep chronicle, I hope enthusiasts will forgive the sometimes brief coverage and hope, like me, that it

might awaken interest and inspire new blood into the restoration movement.

The book is illustrated, in the main, by photographs taken of restored examples which can be seen and touched in the various transport museums today. To younger eyes that have never seen trams or trolley buses or horse-drawn vehicles, such an experience can be quite refreshing, possibly making us a little more grateful for the gleaming car sitting outside our homes.

Stan Yorke

CHAPTER I

The Reluctant Traveller

The weary horses plod across rain-soaked muddy fields that pass for roads in this old engraving from a time when moving goods or people was a venture not to be undertaken lightly.

Prior to the arrival of the high pressure steam engine at the end of the 18th century, there were only two means of travelling – by boat or behind a horse. Both of these methods had been dominated by the need to move goods or livestock and in the 16th century the concept of organized transport available to the public was only just starting. The rich had been able to travel using their own coach and horses but the, so-called, roads were in the main just mud tracks often only used by packhorse trains plodding wearily between towns. Though there is an early reference to a coach in a 13th-century Anglo-Saxon manuscript, little other information about road transport seems to exist until the 1500s. By this period major cities had hard roads and reliable bridges across rivers but away from these centres, roads were still very poor.

By the 1600s we find stage wagons at work, open wagons which carried goods, livestock and passengers, sometimes called carriers' wagons.

Such were the early roads that packhorses were often the only way to transport heavy loads.

Farmers had long given a lift to villagers they knew coming back from a nearby market. The cart, which had taken produce to the market, was empty for the return trip and the villagers who had walked to the market were now returning with goods they had purchased – a perfect arrangement which involved just a few pence in payment.

Then came the stage wagon, and the difference was in the way it operated. Owned by someone whose main business was to provide transport, it covered fixed routes and ran on specific days and you booked your journey, be it for goods or people. Usually driven by a rough, scruffy man wearing dirt-encrusted clothes who may well have originally been a drover, it was relatively slow and for the passengers, open to the weather, and somewhat uncomfortable.

The rural roads were still in a very poor state and crossing rivers posed an enormous problem. In 1555, the Highways Act was passed which established that the repair of roads was the responsibility of the parish. Each parish had to appoint a 'Surveyor of Highways', though the upkeep of river bridges remained with the national authorities. Despite this, improvements were slow in coming. By the early 1600s another attempt was made to improve things by introducing turnpike roads. These were run by trustees who put up money towards improvements and collected tolls from the travellers using the road. Though some trustees failed to achieve any great improvements, the overall road network did slowly improve and the coach services grew steadily through the 17th and 18th centuries. J.L. MacAdam had developed a better road construction system in 1787 which meant at least a consistent technique now existed. An interesting example of the improvements can be seen in the Glasgow to London journey which involved going via Edinburgh. In 1800 this trip took some 13½ days but by 1840 this had become a mere 3½ days.

The same 'run to a timetable' idea was then applied to covered coaches and the stagecoach was born. The 'stage' part of this term referred to the way that the horses were changed every 10 to 15 miles, often at inns where a brief stop would be made to afford refreshment or food, thus breaking the journey down to a number of stages. The drivers of these coaches were, however, the heroes of the day, completely different in appearance and status to the stage wagon drivers. Smartly dressed, the men who drove the crack services were famed for their skill in manoeuvering their coaches. Some of noble birth who had lost their fortunes, usually in gambling, became coachmen, a job that benefited from their skills with horses and their inherent dignity. These coach services had names like The Shuttle, The Commercial, The Sociable, The North Star or The Invincible, an idea to be copied by the railways years later.

The coaches themselves followed a standard design carrying four passengers inside, sometimes squeezing in six, and originally a few more sitting on the roof, their legs simply hanging over the sides. This riding on the roof soon improved by providing basic wooden bench seats until it was common to find up to twelve passengers outside, making a very top heavy coach. So much so that they did occasionally topple over on poor roads. Four horses were normally used and managed some very hard work averaging six or seven miles per hour in summer, though passengers still had to leave the coach and walk up steep hills to reduce the effort needed from the poor animals.

Meanwhile, within the large cities local public transport was about to blossom. In 1625 the first hackney coaches (from the French word *hacquenee* meaning 'a horse for hire') appeared, usually operating from the larger inns. Soon after, the sedan chair arrived to provide personal transport over shorter distances.

The first hackney coaches had two wheels and were pulled by a single horse ridden by the often shabby and dirty driver. Later the outdated or unwanted private coaches of the rich were bought in to provide more room for the passengers. The first hackney coach stand was established in the Strand, London, in 1643, with room for six cabs; the coachman wore a box coat or a caped great coat, knee breeches and a low-crowned hat. In London, opposition from The Watermen's Company, who were losing their monopoly of local transport using the river, kept the cabs at least two miles from the river for several years. By the 1670s a compromise was reached whereby the watermen were employed to supply water for the cab horses and the established hackney cabs became the local transport for most cities.

The sedan chair which seems to have been designed as some form of two man torture. (Transport for London – London Transport Museum Collection)

An ex waterman tending the needs of the horses at a busy hackney coach stand. (London Vintage Taxi Association)

By the end of the 1600s there were 700 licensed hackney coaches in London, now subject to laws and regulations.

Early in the 1800s a variation of the hackney coach appeared where the driver sat on a small seat behind the coach with the reins passing over the passenger carriage. This was called a cabriolet, again a word borrowed from the French, and it was these vehicles that gave us the term 'cab'. 'Hackney' really refers to the vehicle being for hire but as the years went

A modern replica of the later hackney cab. Note the two fold-over covers to protect the occupants' legs. The driver is also definitely up-market. (London Vintage Taxi Association)

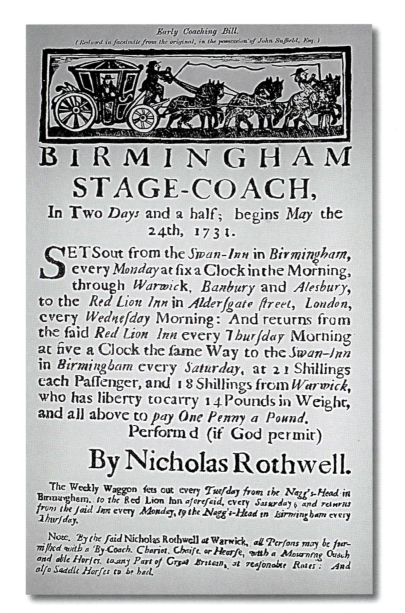

A facsimile of an early 1700s' advertisement for long-distance transport. The stage coach leaves Birmingham at 6 am, and arrives in London on Wednesday morning at a cost of 21 shillings (£1. 05). There was a baggage allowance of 14 lbs; anything over this cost an extra (old) penny per pound weight.

A Royal Mail coach leaving one of the many coaching inns after a brief stop to exchange post and passengers. It probably has a new set of horses as it travels through the snow on the next stage of the journey.

by it tended to apply to four-wheeled coaches whereas two-wheeled carriages were called cabs.

Since 1635 there had been a postal system which used mounted carriers who rode their horses between 'posts' where the postmaster would exchange letters coming and going from his area. Often this would be where the riders would change over in order to rest both the horses and themselves. Frequently the target of robbers, the system was generally very inefficient.

We now stumble on one of those odd cases where an energetic individual causes a massive change. John Palmer

was a theatre owner in Bath and he had adapted the conventional horse-drawn coach to move both actors and equipment between theatres. He approached the Post Office in London with the idea of carrying the post using coaches but met the inevitable disinterest. Not to be put off that easily, he eventually obtained permission from William Pitt, then Chancellor of the Exchequer, to run a test service between London and Bristol in August 1785. Under the old system this had taken 38 hours but using a coach funded by Palmer the trial run took just 16 hours, moving overnight when the roads were virtually empty. Mr Pitt was duly impressed and within a year the service was running to more than ten major towns. Initially the coaches were supplied by independent contractors and carried four passengers inside plus the driver and the heavily armed Post Office guard. The guard was usually recruited from the Army, a background judged most suitable for the job. He stood at the rear of the coach along with the heavy box that contained the post. For the passengers these mail coaches represented the fastest way to travel, only stopping to change the horses and exchange mail. Unlike the passengers and the driver, the guard stayed on for the entire journey and in hard winters it was not unknown for these men to die of hypothermia!

Mr Palmer's zeal was rewarded when he was made the Surveyor and Controller General of the Post Office. In 1787 the Post Office started to develop its own fleet of mail coaches using the best vehicles available (supplied and maintained by John Besant and John Vidler). These were painted in their own distinctive livery of black and scarlet and the driver and guard were resplendent in red uniforms. Due to the demand, seating for a couple of extra passengers was added outside behind the driver.

Before the journey one would have to book at an office where the clerk would enter the details and issue a ticket, not a ticket as we think of it today but a handwritten slip. Should the clerk overbook the coach then he would have to pay out of his own pocket for any extra passenger who needed conveying.

I would like to pause here and look at the horses themselves – their lot was not a happy one. Most horses were hired from a jobmaster by the week, month or year. If you had your own stables and could look after the horse you got the cheapest rates, but a good coach horse would still cost around £100 a year. If the jobmaster stabled them and shoed them it would cost you nearly twice as much. A four-horse coach weighed around a ton with the lightest single-horse coach still weighing around 7 cwt (380 kg). It is generally reckoned that it is working at speed that tires a horse and of course everyone wanted speed. A good horse would be able to cover 14 miles a day, working five days a week. Some of the jobmasters ran several hundred pairs of horses, usually geldings which started in carriage work aged 4½ years old. Out of, say, a thousand horses, a third would leave the stables each year to be auctioned off, their coaching days over, and a further 25 would die from accident or disease. By the 1890s it is estimated that London alone had some 40,000 working horses plus probably as many again in private use.

Thus the idea of public transport had become firmly established, though as always in life, only for those who could afford it.

CHAPTER 2

Enter the Rivals

One of the earliest photos of a railway scene c.1865. It is hard to imagine just what a revolution these machines caused even though they look so antiquated to our modern eyes.

The end of the 18th century saw the growth of the canal system which had been born of the need to move goods, particularly coal. The idea of a fast boat which had priority over normal boats and ran day and night soon developed – the 'fly boat'. These boats had a crew of three or four and usually used two horses which were regularly changed, often without stopping the boat! Pickfords operated one of the best fly boat fleets before transferring their business to the railways. Many of the fly boats would also carry a few passengers and the idea of an express passenger-only service had great appeal. Thus the 'packet boat' service started at the beginning of the 1800s. Given priority over all other boats, they tended to concentrate on providing what today we would call a commuter service in the larger cities. Both fly boats and packet boats operated like the road coaches, running to a timetable and moving day and night. These services were often cheaper than the road vehicles and slightly more comfortable, and usually achieved almost the same speeds.

The next development, however, was to revolutionize public transport and much else besides – the railway had arrived. By 1830 passenger lines were being built and spread like wildfire throughout the land. So great was their effect that by 1850 virtually all the packet boats, passenger-carrying fly boats and the mail coaches, had gone. Incidentally, Glasgow to London now took 15½ hours by train. Road coaches continued to serve towns which had not been reached by the trains and also to provide a service between railway stations and nearby villages. In the large cities they continued in several different forms to provide a commuter service, the precursor to today's buses and taxis. Most had gone by 1914 but some struggled on, with the last London horse cab licence being surrendered in April 1947.

The first railways provided little more than road coaches mounted on flat railway trucks plus open wooden seating for the cheaper seats. As the decades passed, train coaches with comfortable seats arrived and the system settled down. There were three classes, first, second and third, which provided less and less comfort in exchange for cheaper fares. One very important change which was introduced via Parliamentary pressure was the idea of very cheap 'workmen's' tickets, though these were usually confined to very early and late trains.

The Victorian era saw political manoeuvering reach ever higher levels. The railway companies had quickly grown into vast empires with considerable influence and they were often accused of holding back the development of road transport.

We must, however, remember that vast amounts of invested money had

A modern-day replica of an early Liverpool & Manchester train, with most definitely first class coaches. Note the road coach shape outlined in black to give passengers confidence in the new means of travel.

An early coach, with only four rigid wheels and no way of moving from one coach to another. These were still a big improvement over the very early, open coaches, however.

been spent in creating a network which, by 1880, could claim to have a railway within 15 miles of virtually every town in England. To start investing in a rival road system when there were only horse-drawn vehicles to use it, seemed folly. The railway companies could also make a good case for Government support. They were commercial companies who had to have satisfied several government inquiries just to get the Act they needed before they could even start, indeed most applications to build a railway failed. But not only had they to purchase the land the tracks covered, but they were also responsible for the thousands of miles of fencing and any bridges needed to pass over or under established roads. Road transport, on the other hand, paid paltry tolls for the roads and certainly cared not a jot

for any idea of protecting people or animals from their activities.

Even though we had used stagecoaches for many decades, the arrival in the 1840s and 1850s of a transport system that moved 50 or 100 people at a time, could travel safely at 30 or 40 mph and generally ran reliably come rain or shine, was a revolution. In the first few decades the railways saw their job as covering medium to long distances. Virtually every stop had a station building with staff to help passengers with luggage and tickets. The station quickly became a well known point even if, because of the geography, it was a mile or two from the town or village. Horse-drawn carts and coaches plied regularly between station and town and it was now practical to visit the local city and return within the day.

The vast spread of train travel brought interesting challenges. The first was time-keeping. At the start of the 1800s time was still set by noting midday by the position of the sun – just as a sundial would show. This meant that midday in London was not the same as midday in, say, Bristol. It was the railways that needed a universal time based on London and indeed it was originally called 'London Time'. The other problem was the time and delay caused by issuing handwritten tickets or 'bills'. A stationmaster on the Newcastle & Carlisle Railway, one Thomas Edmondson, devised a system in the 1840s based on pre-printed card

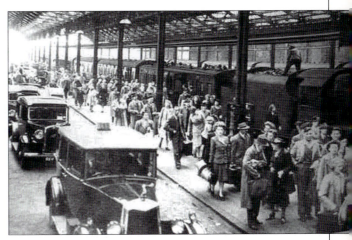

This scene at Llandudno station in the early 1940s was a common sight on summer Saturdays as holidaymakers escaped from the towns to the seaside in the days when motor cars were scarce and the price of railway travel was within the reach of the working classes. (John Powell)

Edmondson tickets were printed on a stiff card nearly 1 mm thick. Today, the preserved steam railways still issue similar tickets.

tickets. Each bore the journey details, the cost and the class. Though his employers were not interested, the Manchester & Leeds Company were and adopted his idea. Edmondson formed a company to supply the tickets and the machines that stamped the date across the end of the ticket, the only action the booking clerk needed to do. The Edmondson ticket system became standard on the railways and indeed made his family a fortune courtesy of a simple royalty system. Within the booking office there would be racks of these pre-printed tickets plus blank ones that could be filled in by hand for the occasional unusual journey. A similar idea was later used on the buses and trams.

Throughout the 19th century the railways were still run by independent companies, some small and local, others large with hundreds of miles of track. Inevitably, popular inter-city journeys were offered by separate companies using their own tracks to and from their own stations. Most cities and large industrial towns had two or three stations owned by different companies and the intense rivalry drove improvements forward. Speeds continued to climb – 50, 60 and even 70 mph were regularly reached well before the turn of the century. Passenger comfort also improved: coaches with corridors and toilets appeared, as did restaurant coaches and buffets, and the trains grew longer, now carrying several hundred people. The need for toilets

'All change for Cheltenham!' A larger rural station or possibly a junction would have had extensive facilities for handling goods as well as passengers. In winter there would have been a coal fire roaring in the waiting room grate and quite often refreshments as well, just as the coaching inns had provided 100 years before.

Country stations from a different era. Even a small village stop like this would have had a porter, a station master and a signalman. Often restrained from getting close to a small village by the local geography, these stations relied on their passengers walking to the station to catch the train or being delivered by horse-drawn vehicles. It's easy to see why these stations were the first to close once the country buses arrived.

was to avoid having to stop expresses regularly and the corridor was simply to enable passengers to reach the toilets.

On the lines around the southern side of London the novel idea of commuter trains had developed along with stations every mile or so. Very soon the other major companies followed and the idea spread throughout the land. Journeys of up to 30 miles, on which there might well be 15 or more stations, started to appear and this led to a massive development of suburban areas plus the commuter town. The so-called 'Metroland' development by the Metropolitan Railway in London personifies this movement and by the 1920s trains carried hundreds of thousands into the cities and back every day. This had coincided with the vast expansion of the middle classes who could afford the better housing and the fares to travel from their rural haven to town for work.

The long-distance main line routes reached a zenith in the 1930s with superb steam engines accomplishing journey times that motor buses and coaches could only dream of. The quieter rural lines, however, were already failing to compete with the new motor bus, whilst only desperate overcrowding on the roads kept the suburban trains alive.

There was one variation on the conventional railways that was built to ease the traffic congestion in London – the Underground. These lines were originally built just below street level and indeed were often under the roads themselves. The cuttings were dug, given brick walls and then the 'top' put back on. They had to manoeuvre around the existing drains and buried rivers – indeed, the

old Fleet river crosses over the lines (District and Circle), in pipes, in the middle of Victoria station. Originally pulled by steam locomotives, they were electrified using a four-rail system: two conventional rails on which the train ran and two rails for the electricity supply and return. All these lines connected with the normal railways away from the city centre. When yet more underground lines were deemed necessary they had to be taken much deeper to avoid the ever-increasing electricity, gas, water and telephone lines. This extra depth meant that true tunnel construction was needed and the 'tube' system was

A typical corridor on a main line train which any Harry Potter fan will recognise. Each compartment had its own sliding door and offered much more comfort than any previous public transport.

born. It also meant that the routes were no longer tied to being under the roads, it was now feasible to route the lines according to the anticipated demand. Special electric trains were designed to fit the smaller bore of the tunnels whilst still using the standard running rail gauge. Amazing numbers of passengers are carried to this day by the Underground and Tube lines, which because of their city centre location came under London Transport administration, along with the buses, trolleys and trams. Though not on the London scale, several other cities built underground routes which still run today.

A London underground train (left) and the smaller tube train (right). Note the unusual four rail system.

We have, however, got a little ahead of ourselves as the same developments of materials and engineering were appearing in older, traditional road transport systems.

Main line stations were always very atmospheric – the echoing steps on hard floors, the drifting steam from the engines and the very special sounds that were quite unique. This painting by Marjorie Sherlock is of London's Liverpool Street station in the 1920s. (National Railway Museum/Science & Society Picture Library)

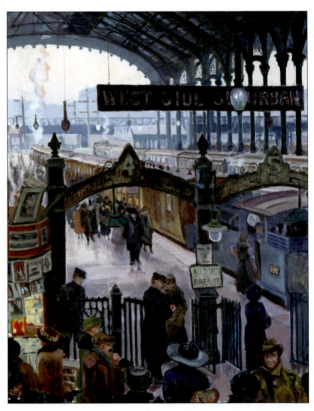

CHAPTER 3

Bigger is Better

Ludgate Hill in London showing a wonderful mix of open carriages, horse-drawn carts and early motor buses. There's even a train crossing the bridge to complete the scene.

Engineers have always experimented, trying to devise better, bigger or faster machines and the world of transport was no exception. In 1802 Trevithick, the famous Cornish engineer, had built a small high pressure steam engine which he applied to moving a road coach. Unfortunately, its weight combined with the narrow, solid wheels proved too much for the crude road surfaces of the day. He turned instead to making steam engines that could pull mineral wagons along simple tracks, a task previously performed by a horse. The rest, as they say, is history!

During the first decades of the 1800s the horse-drawn coach had taken a major step in the 'make it bigger' direction. Still only found within the large cities where the roads were relatively good, we see the arrival from France of what could just about be called the first buses. These still retained the four-wheel arrangement of earlier coaches with the rear wheels

Shillibeers' first 'bus' centenary was celebrated in 1929 by the construction of this replica coach, seen here at a much later date in London. The use of three horses was unusual and later was dropped in favour of just two. (Transport for London – London Transport Museum Collection)

larger than the front and employing two or three horses to pull them. It was the size and shape of the carriage that changed, getting longer and having an overall roof. These services, pioneered by John Greenwood in Manchester and George Shillibeer in London, carried up to 22 people, all seated. The London coaches which started in 1829 ran from Paddington to Bank, could be boarded along the route and had a conductor who collected the fares. This justified the name of omnibuses, again from France and meaning 'for all'. Just three years later the State Carriage Act was passed which legalized the stopping to collect passengers anywhere on the route and the number of these 'bus' services started to grow apace.

The ability to produce small steam engines, however, kept the engineers busy and the 1830s saw the start of steam-engined omnibuses. In 1831 a steam engine pulled a passenger trailer between Cheltenham and Gloucester and a similar system was introduced between London and Greenwich in 1833. The same year saw Walter Hancock start a twelve-seater steam bus service in competition with Shillibeer's horse-drawn buses but the machinery wasn't quite ready – the service lasted just

A painting of three of Hancock's steam-driven coaches. As so often, the artist has neglected the rather important mechanical parts so we are left to assume that there was room at the rear for an engine driver cum fireman.

An example of the slightly later horse-drawn bus with forward-facing upstairs seating. The downstairs seats would remain positioned along the sides of the bus for many decades until the wider motor-driven bus arrived. These buses needed considerable skill to drive as there was only a single wooden brake block bearing onto the rim of the larger wheel on each side. (This bus is on display in the Manchester Transport Museum.)

two weeks. Undaunted, Hancock was soon back and by 1836 he had two larger steam-engined vehicles in use; one had 18 seats, the other held 22. At the same time a 26-seat steam bus started between Glasgow and Paisley. The public viewed these vehicles with some caution, fearing that the boiler might explode, just as sometimes happened at this time on the railways, albeit very rarely.

I have mentioned how the arrival of the railways ended the long distance coach services, but in large towns and cities the need for local transport to and from the stations

A replica Derby Tramways Company horse bus, seen here in the 800-year celebrations in Derby in 1954. (www.picturethepast. org.uk)

saw a big increase in both horse-drawn and steam-engined buses. Such was the demand for these local services that passengers started to climb onto the bus roof if the inside was full, just as had happened 200 years earlier on the original smaller stagecoaches. By 1850 this practice was accepted and the buses had a ladder at the rear and simple seats on the roof. Initially these were two long bench seats placed back to back along the centre of the roof, such that the passengers looked out over the sides of the bus. Known as a 'knifeboard', the arrangement had two problems. If the bus jerked or turned a little too fast, passengers could be simply thrown over the edge of the roof. The second problem concerned ladies, who were somewhat exposed, indeed they would rarely ever go on the top of these buses. Both these difficulties were alleviated by fitting a so-called 'decency board' along each side of the roof and the ladder was replaced by a narrow spiral stairway. Before long these boards were used to carry advertisements and indeed buses have had adverts in roughly the same place ever since. In 1881 the first bus was built with the 'upstairs' seats facing forwards, so-called 'garden

seats', though there was still no cover or roof over the upstairs area.

These changes were applied to both horse-drawn and steam-driven buses but the horse-drawn bus remained far and away the most common vehicle. In the 1890s Mr Purnell Hooley of Northampton had developed Tarmac, a mixture of ironstone slag and tar which was more waterproof than the older surfacing and produced a smoother road surface. Its use to improve the roads was paid for by a tax on cars and fuel!

The logistics of operating vast fleets of horse-drawn buses in the large cities was a considerable task, involving bringing in food, straw and hay, and employing farriers to shoe the horses and vets to tend to their health. Taking figures from the London General Omnibus Company, the largest bus company serving the largest city, we can get a glimpse of just how busy these support activities were. It had some 600 buses and 6,000 horses; the typical bus would cover around 60 miles a day with the horses working for three to four hours. The company contracted eight vets and 25 farriers and had enormous stables. A horse would last for about four years in this work though some worked for seven or eight years before being retired. A constant supply of food was brought to a central mill in Paddington by canal boats whilst hay was brought in by horse-drawn carts direct to the various depots. The omnibuses themselves lasted for ten years during which time the wheels would have been completely replaced three or four times and the iron tyres which took the hammering of running on the road surface were renewed every three or four months. One rather odd aspect of the early omnibuses was the absence of any route information. The route was in fact indicated by the colour scheme of the bus and not the lettering, which was restricted to the sides and included the name of the operating company, the destination and, as ever, advertising.

The last horse-drawn bus in London photographed in 1914. Many of the bus and tram horses were commandeered for use in the First World War and this could well have been the fate for this pair.

CHAPTER 4

The Era of the Tram

This view taken in Manchester around 1900 shows an open-top, four-wheel tram, plus several horse-drawn carriages and carts. There are plenty of pedestrians about but the odd thing to modern eyes is that there are no cars!

Today we tend to think of trams as a modern answer to the problems of overcrowded cities, always electric and invariably enshrined in terms like 'Metro'. Strictly these systems are light railways spending a relatively small proportion of their journey on streets. On the Continent the tram never disappeared and today networks of sleek trams fill the centres of many major cities. So first a definition – the key feature is that a tram runs on rails and shares normal roads. Over the years it has been pulled by a steam locomotive or horses, or has had built-in electric motors powered via the rails or overhead wires or even batteries. Part of its charm lies in the delightful Victorian shape and style which stayed with the tram right through to its final death throes in 1962. It lived through the age of photography and is thus well recorded and today restored trams can still be seen in action. Always painted in elaborate colour schemes and covered with advertisements, they are instinctively attractive.

The tram had actually arrived from America in 1860 when one George Francis Train opened his 'street railway' in Birkenhead. A year later he had three tramways open in London but these were met with less than enthusiasm. The rails he used projected above the road surface and were a serious problem to wheeled vehicles – that is to say, everybody else using the road! Two of his routes ran past the houses of the rich, where there really was no need for public transport, and being an American didn't help either. Within the year all had gone, indeed trams never again ran over these two unsuitable London routes. In our strangely class-conscious land the tram was always seen as working class and following its rather faltering start in London it faced opposition throughout its hundred year life.

Though the industrial revolution was virtually over by the 1850s the resultant technical knowledge had driven a manufacturing revolution that was now just getting into full swing; already over half the population lived in towns and worked in factories. Throughout the next 50 years the population increased at an alarming rate, as did factories and the coal, iron and steel industries that fed them. Bradford is a good example, going from 13,000 souls in 1800 to 104,000 by 1850 and then to 280,000 by 1900. Many other industrial cities followed a similar rate of expansion. The need for transport had never been greater and despite wars and occasional depressions this era saw the peak in transport development. The horse-drawn tram was central to the need to move people to and from the factories and its expansion was spectacular, as a few figures show:

Year	Mileage	Horses	Passengers
1878	270	9,000	146,000,000
1882	560	18,000	258,000,000
1890	950	27,000	526,000,000

Trams provided early services, typically starting at 5 am or soon after, and workmen's tickets, valid until 7 am, would cost half the normal fare. Fares were in any case very reasonable and strangely changed very little after 1900 right up to the 1950s.

Between 1862 and the 1870s tramways were built in almost every industrial town of any size, though London had to wait until 1870 to get its first lines after Mr Train had left. All the lines now used grooved rails which were flush with the road surface.

Trams could be heavier than the omnibuses due to their using smooth track rather than the rough road surfaces, and were built in two sizes: small, around 1½ tons with 14 to 18 passengers and pulled by a single horse, or large at 2½ tons with 42 to 46 passengers and using two horses.

Road omnibuses using two or three horses were generally limited to a maximum of 24 passengers and extra horses were added to climb hills, called 'chain horses' as chains were used to link them to the original shaft; steep hills might require up to five extra. Horses used on hilly routes would be regularly rotated to work on flatter routes to help them recover.

A small section of tram track. The wheels ran on the wide top section whilst the thin section acted as a barrier to the road materials.

When a curve was needed, the track was bent using this fearsome gadget and a great deal of physical strength.

Most early trams used the American Brill trucks. This is a 21E truck of 1899.

Steam engine-drawn road vehicles had faded during this period, mainly due to the Locomotive on Highways Act of 1865 which required any mechanically drawn vehicle to be limited to 4 mph and preceded down the road by a person carrying a red flag. This law had been encouraged by the powerful railway companies who realized all too well that steam road travel could damage their business. Modified in 1878, it wasn't repealed until 1896.

We are now approaching the decades when all the scientific

A typical horse-drawn tram with garden seats upstairs; in many ways a larger version of the older horse-drawn coach.

work that had been quietly going on for most of the Victorian age suddenly bore fruit in the field of transport.

Initially tram operators simply sought to increase the speeds, particularly on acceleration and hill climbing. The first idea was to replace the horse with a small steam engine, but combining it within the tram itself proved difficult and the idea was soon dropped in favour of a separate locomotive pulling a traditional tramcar. The first example in a major city was in Glasgow in 1877, though the locomotive was bound by Board of Trade regulations and looked like a small plain tram with no mechanisms showing beyond its chimney. To meet the city's requirements they burnt coke (less smoke) and condensed the

A lovingly-restored, horse-drawn tram on display outside the workshops of the Manchester Transport Museum Society in Heaton Park in north Manchester. Until 1970 it had been used as a fish and chip shop! This 'Eades' L53 reversible tram was built in Manchester around 1880.

exhaust steam back to water for re-use to avoid having to carry too much water. They also had to be relatively quiet. Compared to horses it cost almost 20 times as much but it could run for 70 miles a day, easily maintain 6 mph and could tackle hills unaided, well, nearly always. The tram itself could now be bigger, carrying some 60 passengers, and had a roof over the windswept upper deck. Smoke and smuts from the chimney caused some problems but the roof kept these to a minimum. The heavier load meant that the old four-wheel design couldn't cope and so, like railway coaches, the tram car was mounted on two bogies. This spread the load but still permitted turning through the tight radius curves abundant at the city road junctions.

The steam tram was particularly popular in the Midlands and the North with over 500 locomotives in use at its peak around 1890. A few

(Above) A steam-drawn tram shuffles along a snow-covered street in Birmingham and (below), a restored Beyer Peacock tram locomotive originally built in 1880.

A famous example of the rural tramway which lasted way beyond its time – the Brill tramway in Buckinghamshire. It eventually closed in 1935 after a few years as part of the London Transport Underground network.

rural tramways carried on with worn out locomotives and tram cars into the 1920s, long after they disappeared from the towns and cities. The steam-hauled tram introduced the idea of stopping at set points – tram stops, whereas previously a horse-drawn tram would stop as needed.

There was, of course, nothing technically new in these machines, but waiting just around the corner were electricity, petrol and diesel.

We must mention one short-lived variation: the cable-hauled tram which almost by definition excelled at climbing hills, as it still does in San Francisco and Llandudno in North Wales. The principle is simple. An endless cable moves along in a slot between the two running rails, and at the ends it passes around a large pulley or drum which is driven, originally by a steam engine, and provides the energy. Each tram or locomotive has a 'gripper' which reaches down into the slot and holds onto the moving cable. The grip can be released to allow the tram to stop and then be reapplied to continue. The cable moves continuously at around 8 mph and thus imparts a constant speed to the trams, be they going uphill, downhill or round corners. Disadvantage number one is that the friction of dragging the cable along consumes 50% of the power! Not an unbearable problem since the engine driving the cable runs at a constant speed and can be optimized for this. Problem number two, though, was the system's downfall. The cable only lasted about a year and was difficult to replace and expensive. It also sometimes broke, leaving the line in chaos. Very occasionally one of the grippers would jam in the 'grip'

Point work on the Llandudno system showing that only one movable blade is used (near the red mark). The square plates are a vital part of cable systems giving access to the pulleys that steer the cable around the curves.

position and this simply meant that the hapless tram continued to move until it hit the next tram which had released its gripper and stopped to let passengers on and off.

Cable tramways were built in many places – the first, in 1884, plied up and down Highgate Hill in London. By the mid 1890s there were systems in south London, Birmingham, Edinburgh and Matlock in Derbyshire. Most changed to electric trams early in the 20th century but Edinburgh held on until 1923, whilst the short Matlock system made it into 1927. Today the Great Orme tramway still shows what they were like as it lifts its passengers high above the streets of Llandudno, though this system doesn't use a gripper, it simply has a car permanently attached at each end of the cable, the winding gear

changing direction to enable each tram to rise and then return.

Early work on electric traction had been carried out in Germany and America and in 1883 Magnus Volk opened an electric railway along the beach in Brighton (a small section of

Not California but Llandudno in North Wales, with one of the two single cable cars descending towards the town. It is no mean achievement to operate a system such as this within today's strict health and safety regulations, and there has been extensive rebuilding in recent years.

which still runs). Busy looking at these systems were the tramway engineers and one initial problem they had to solve was how to get the electric power safely to the tram. A third rail hidden in a slot down the centre of the line was used on the very first electric tram opened in Blackpool in 1885. There were difficulties keeping the 'conduit' dry and free from rubbish, though this type of system was still in use in the early 1950s. It had been adopted mainly in London on the large London County Council system but was always expensive to maintain. In 1891 the system that was to become the norm was tried out in Leeds: the overhead wire. High enough above the roadway, the dangerous high voltage feed wire was out of reach and relatively easy to hold in place from tall standards placed along the road. A good team of workers could erect 20 to 30 poles (standards) in a day and later the wires could be installed with distances of over half a mile being erected in a day. Inevitably there were objectors to these, claiming they disfigured the view, and all manner of Victorian brackets and scrolls were added to decorate the otherwise plain poles.

A more serious problem was that the return electric current wandered from the ground level tracks and shared its journey down underground telephone cables, gas pipes and water pipes. Hard work

and better return cables reduced this until by 1900 most objections had subsided leaving the way for massive conversion to electric traction. This same problem of stray electric currents in the ground was cited as one of the main reasons to end trams in the 1950s and 1960s. There was one other financial worry that held the enthusiastic rush in check. Tramways were often built with a clause that enabled the local authorities to purchase the line after 21 years, and many of the lines' companies who were anxious to upgrade were very close to this limit. The problem was that the purchase was optional, so who was going to invest large sums of money before they knew if the council would take up the option to purchase?

Two double deck trams using the Kingsway tram tunnel in London. Like much of central London the routes used the conduit system of collecting the electricity. The slot can just be made out between the running rails and a 'plough' hung down under the tram and into the conduit below this slot. Here two large contacts slid along two electrified rails.

By 1896 we had 50 miles of electrified tramways but in America there were over 12,000 miles and thus much of the early tram equipment either came from America or was based on their designs.

Tramways that did become municipal concerns between 1892 and 1900 included Plymouth, Leeds, Sheffield, Liverpool, Aberdeen and Sunderland. Some towns anxious to be 'modern' built their tramway with the intention of leasing the operation to private companies but there were no bidders so the councils had to take on the running themselves; Huddersfield was the first in 1882. By 1900 municipal-owned systems were carrying 70% of all passengers and by 1937 this figure was 95%.

Despite these worries, line after line converted to overhead wires and electric trams. Glasgow followed in 1898 with London, Birmingham and Manchester changing to overhead electric power in 1901.

The electric motors could impart more energy to the wheels than horses and thus the electric tram was usually larger and heavier than its predecessor necessitating laying new, stronger track. Most electric trams were purpose-built, but some of the locomotive-hauled tramcars were converted horse cars. Many early electric trams were double deck, with the upper deck open to the sky, but slowly trams with a fully covered upper deck became standard. Single deck trams were also used on less busy routes. There is one story from the Halifax area concerning the line to Queensbury, which ran over high and bleak land between the towns. Here, covered trams plied the route in summer but in winter they would be

A Portsmouth Corporation tram showing great faith in the English weather. Not only does it have an open top but the driver has to stand in the open all day. (Milestones)

replaced by open top trams in what might seem a strangely masochistic move. The reason was simply that the worst of the winter winds had actually blown the occasional covered tram over whereas the, presumably empty, uncovered upstairs allowed the gales to pass through.

The operation of a tram poses a problem when it reaches the end of

Maintaining the overhead wires required a special vehicle. On this horse-drawn version, the platform can be elevated by means of two cables which are wound up.

There were many variations on the degree of shelter the trams afforded. This Leicester model has open ends to the upper deck and the driver still gets frozen in winter. It worked from 1904 until 1947.

the route – how to turn around? Many routes ended in a tight radius loop so the tram carried on in the same direction. Sometimes this loop was formed by using the existing streets, giving an apparent one-way operation for a short distance. For many routes this luxury couldn't be provided so the pole collecting the electricity was pulled down using a long pole (stored in a tube beneath the tram), swung around the tram in a half circle and then raised to reconnect to the overhead wire but now facing back the way it had come. This operation could be quite tricky as the pulley at the end of the roof pole had to be aimed very carefully or it simply missed the wire. This would still leave all the upstairs seats facing backwards on the return journey so the back rests would be flipped over, effecting a complete reversal of the seat. The downstairs seats were usually set out against the sides of the tram facing each other, which left a good space for standing passengers. Virtually all electric trams had driving positions at both ends and were visually identical whichever way they were travelling.

Surprisingly, there were some areas that never had electric trams – Oxford, Cambridge, the West End and the City of London, for example. Many systems extended their lines out to the edges of the towns to encourage developers to build; indeed it was often claimed that the value of property on these outer suburbs doubled when the electric trams arrived. Some routes ventured out to truly rural areas and reached far enough to join the system from an adjacent city. Unfortunately some councils were very parochial and would refuse to consider through-running, a feature that the soon-to-arrive motor buses would exploit. In several areas there were systems of different gauges – Yorkshire in particular had four different gauges in use, preventing through running between many of its towns. An example would be the eleven-mile journey from Bradford to Huddersfield via Halifax which involved three different companies and three changes of gauge (4ft, 3ft 6in and lastly 4ft 8½ in). Nevertheless, by 1914 there were 13,000 trams operating over 2,500 miles of tramways.

Tram operators soon realized the need for mass movement of people to events like football matches and on Sundays to favourite countryside spots. Just one year after opening, the trams in Bristol carried some 30,000 people just going to the country on the

The slightly easier way is to use a rope which enables the pole to be pulled down and walked around the tram before returning it to the overhead wire.

Changeover seat backs on the seats of a single deck tram. These open-sided trams were reserved for summer use and served on seaside routes.

My favourite restored tram from the Sheffield fleet. It manages to combine an almost Art Nouveau feel with the traditional rugged tram. Its history is somewhat more complex having been sold to Gateshead where it was modified. Later the lower part survived as a garden shed until restored with a 'new' Sheffield top.

the days before the private motor car and a large proportion of fans would use the trams, the rest would walk or use a bicycle. Music halls were also catered for; London for instance had some 500 such halls entertaining an estimated 300,000 people every night – late night tram services to such places were obviously very busy. Many towns ran special services at 11 pm every evening just to take home the somewhat merry drinkers when the pubs closed.

Liverpool attempted to break the historic association with the working class by introducing 'first class only' trams in 1908. More expensive but with upholstered seats, they ran on routes that served better-off regions and lasted until 1923.

Whilst the arrival of electricity (incidentally then still generated by each town's own power station) had

August bank holiday. Many football stadiums had long sidings into which visiting trams would cram and then await the equally mad rush when the match ended. Remember these were

An unusual shot from the workshops in the Crich Tram Museum. The rebuilt electric motor has been replaced into the refurbished truck as part of an extensive restoration job.

Two more examples of the electric tram in its heyday: (above) from Glasgow, now fully enclosed and fitted with bogies to achieve greater length and seating capacity. Note the use of a 'bow' collector rather than the usual pulley wheel to collect the electricity. This allowed the tram to pass complex overhead layouts without risking the pole leaving the wires.

(Right) The maximum weight that could be carried by a basic four-wheel truck. You will probably notice the slatted wooden life guards mounted near ground level to prevent dogs or children from crawling under the trams whilst stationary. This is a Leeds city tram from 1925 carrying passengers at the Crich Tram Museum.

given the tram a massive boost, petrol and diesel fuels were giving birth to the public transport vehicles that would soon deliver a fatal blow to trams and inflict lasting damage to the trains as well.

This same period saw the railways adopt electric traction, principally for the intensely used commuter lines. The underground systems also changed over from steam to electricity, to the general relief of the passengers!

The 1890 to 1925 period can seem very odd to modern eyes. The vast increase in the population had meant that all the rival public transport systems survived together – the commuter railways, the trams, horse-drawn omnibuses and, as we shall see in the next chapter, the petrol engine buses. Medium and long journeys were still dominated by trains but with the ever improving roads, horse-drawn coaches continued to ply over surprisingly long routes. The petrol engine had appeared and the private motor car existed, but few in number and still a rich man's toy.

Another restored tram which runs on the system in Heaton Park. This line ran from the Manchester suburbs and was packed in summer and at weekends with people simply going out for a walk in this enormous park.

CHAPTER 5

The Bus Comes of Age

Rivals passing! The times they are a'changing – the motor bus on the right looks well patronised, and there are two other motor vehicles in sight.

Throughout this same era the horse-drawn omnibus was still at work, occasionally mixing with the mad rush of the cities. Like the first horse-drawn trams, what it lacked was speed and size. I want to look at a few variations which were not to last too long but added interest to this eventful period.

Though the steam engine had been tried built into trams, it now reappeared more successfully in buses. Experiments had started in 1897 with buses made by Lifu and in 1902 a 36-seater Thornycroft steam bus was trialled. During this period, two makes dominated, being used in several places including London: the

French Darracq-Serpollets and from Colchester, the Clarkson steam buses. The French vehicles employed a flash boiler (no, it's not a modern idea!) which reduced the risk of the boiler exploding.

Another interesting idea which has reappeared in different forms several times in recent years was the petrol-electric bus. In this a petrol engine drove an electricity generator which in turn fed electric motors which powered the bus. The most successful were built by Hallfors-Stevens and put into service by Thomas Tilling. One of the reasons for their popularity was the difficulty drivers had with the still-crude manual gearboxes and clutches on the petrol engines, whilst the petrol/electric vehicle was much easier to control.

Originally from the 1920s, this much restored Sentinel steam bus regularly gives rides at transport events, seen here at a Fleetwood Tram Day event.

A 1915 Tillings-Stevens petrol electric bus from the Worthing area, resplendent in the Amberley Museum where it is still operational. These buses were not great at climbing hills but had a surprisingly long life in service for what was, after all, a specialised vehicle.

There were also battery vehicles, quiet but always plagued by their limited range due to the need to recharge the batteries. The earliest was introduced in 1889 by the Ward Electrical Car Company, followed two years later by W.C. Bersey who employed a 26-seater double deck battery bus between Victoria and Charing Cross. Liverpool also saw similar vehicles provided by the Electric Motive Power Company. Their weight was also high due to the massive battery cells, which usually weighed in at more than a ton, but they introduced the idea of a propeller shaft driving the rear axle via a bevel gear rather than the chain drive still standard on petrol-engined vehicles. A short-lived revival occurred in the First World War when Edison produced a small single deck, battery-powered bus which was used in Derby, Lancaster, Southend, South Shields, West Bromwich and York, but this was the last development of this type of vehicle until the 1970s.

A battery bus on charge before its next journey. These vehicles were always hampered by the weight of the batteries.

For a while all these variations could be found competing with the tram and the still busy horse-drawn vehicles. The petrol engine (and later the diesel engine) though, were to eventually triumph, sweeping all before them.

Around 1900 several petrol engine-driven buses were tried in Torquay, Blackpool, Newport Pagnell and London; even the Hon C.S. Rolls tried out an imported single deck Canstatt-Daimler. In 1902 the London Motor Omnibus Syndicate started a service from Marble Arch using small twelve-seater Scott-Stirling buses. Within two years both Thomas Tilling and the Birch Brothers had started petrol bus services into central London and by 1905 there were 20 such buses at work, many of these made by Milnes-Daimler.

Petrol-engined bus services outside London included Southampton in 1901, and Eastbourne and Cornwall in 1903. Most were used to run to and from railway stations.

In 1908 the London General Omnibus Company joined several new companies who between them were now running over 1,000 vehicles. Just one year later the General, as it became known, had absorbed many of its rivals. It soon started to build its own buses at Walthamstow, or at least the bodies as the chassis and engines were usually built by specialist companies. At this time there were many different companies making engines and chassis, mostly on the Continent, plus just as many building the bodies. The use of a chain drive meant the bus floor was over 2 ft above the road, resulting in many

An early Thorneycroft bus on display in the Milestones Museum. Note the handle for starting the engine, the solid tyres and the life guard boards still needed because of the height of the vehicle above the road.

having a wooden guard between the wheels to deter inquisitive children. These early buses, though, were far from perfect and filled the crowded city roads with noise and obnoxious blue fumes.

Progress in London was also held back by the Metropolitan Police who would not allow double deck buses to have a roof over the upper floor in case the extra weight toppled the bus, and speeds were held down to 12 mph. Despite this the engineers continued to push forward and in 1910 the Daimler Company produced a double decker with a roof and an under-floor engine, a feature destined to become standard on single deck

buses and coaches many years later.

The collecting of fares posed a massive problem for trams and buses. The need to take the money and then to be able to check that passengers had paid for the ride they were taking had been solved for the railways by the card ticket. On trams and buses the process had to be carried out at great speed; unlike the trains, buses stopped every minute or so. There was no way the conductor could carry pre-printed tickets for every possible journey so a different technique was developed which relied on the conductor knowing his route. He carried a set of pre-printed tickets of fixed values. Around the outside edges were printed the numbers of the various

Tram and bus tickets and the almost universal Bell ticket punch.

Delivered in 1925, probably on solid tyres, this Dennis 4-ton bus was sold to the London General Omnibus Co in 1926 but scrapped by 1930. It laid in storage for 39 years before being rediscovered and completely restored. It has visited Japan, worked for the English Tourist Board, featured in films and TV shows, and is now lovingly tended by the Cobham Bus Museum.

stages that the route was divided into. In response to the passenger stating their destination, the conductor would remember the fare from where the journey started to the destination, draw out the appropriate priced ticket and then punch a hole through the stage number where the passenger had boarded the bus, or sometimes the destination stage. The ticket in effect said you may travel as far as the price allows from the stage number where you boarded. It was relatively easy to issue and easy to check as well.

The conductors kept the takings for the day and would pay them in when they arrived for duty at the depot the next day. There was considerable fiddling though and to help counter this, the punches used by the conductors had a box which stored the small round bit of ticket that had been punched out. The bus companies also employed undercover 'passengers' who would note the numbers of people on the journey to give at least some hope of confirming the number of tickets that should have been issued. One famous lady who was employed in this task could recite the entire journey's activities, stop by stop. Despite this the bus and tram companies lived with an estimated annual loss of around £25,000 from ticket fraud.

The First World War caused massive changes, as horse-drawn buses lost their animals to the war effort. Technology was also pushing forward and the 1920s saw a steady

Another single deck bus from 1927 – the Leyland 'Lion'. This had a 5.1 litre petrol engine and like the others in this section now ran on pneumatic tyres. This one is in Ribble colours and though a great advance in their day the buses are difficult to maintain and drive. To be able to see these early restored buses moving is a real treat.

improvement in buses and trams plus a new rival – the trolley bus. One unexpected effect of the war was that many returning ex-servicemen received a lump sum payment and finding there were no jobs or work, some used the money to start small local bus services, often with just one converted ex-army vehicle. They deliberately sought out places and routes which were busy, to the alarm of the big companies and though many of these failed very quickly it heralded a period of large numbers of small companies which at least kept the big boys on their toes.

Now the horses had gone, the roads were free from the endless sea of loose nails dropped from

A lovely example of a 'Queen' bus built by Midland Red in 1927 and supplied to several operators, this one being for Northern General Transport. These were only just over 4 tons in weight and carried 37 passengers in their modest 25 feet length; over 650 were built.

horseshoes and buses could begin to use the new pneumatic tyres developed by Dunlop in 1916. Introduced in London in 1928, buses so fitted were allowed to travel at the unprecedented speed of 20 mph. By the late 1930s seats were upholstered and better engines gave greater comfort, confidence and speed. Even the driver's cab had windows and a windscreen. The other more subtle change was the gradual increase in vehicle width. This allowed the seats to be set in pairs facing forward and thus increase the number of passengers carried.

The medium-distance coach appeared using first petrol engines and, in the 1930s, diesel. These were simply single deck buses but with more attention to comfort and sustained speeds.

One of the early diesel engine buses, an AEC 'Regent' from 1934.

This is Midland Red's first double deck bus, with a fully covered roof. When a new model was introduced it had to be tested for stability and this rather dangerous process was undertaken by the manufacturer (Short Bros. in this case). Note the ropes ready to catch the bus should it topple.

Another remarkably modern-looking bus from the 1930s. A 54-seat Daimler of 1937 vintage – one of some 800 purchased by Birmingham Corporation and which finally ended service in 1959. These buses had a 7-litre Gardner diesel engine with a pre-selector gear box which saved much effort for the driver. (On display at the Birmingham and Midland Museum of Transport)

CHAPTER 6

The Trolley Bus

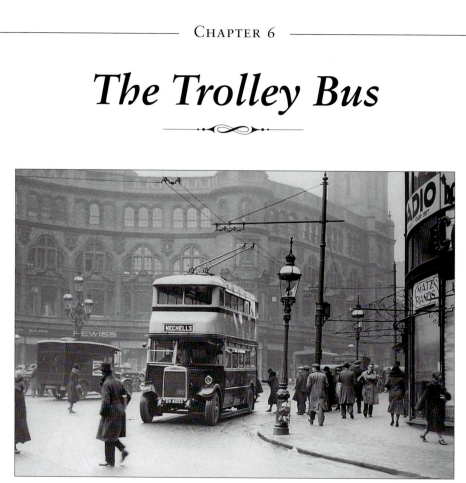

The first trolley bus route in the West Midlands from Birmingham centre to Nechells with a Leyland bodied four-wheeled trolley photographed in 1932. Note the absence of any tram lines and the glorious gas lamps.

Anyone watching the development of the electric tram in the 1890s would have soon wondered why it had to run on rails – why not take the horse bus and simply replace the horse with electric traction? Dr Werner Von Siemens had demonstrated an electric vehicle, which took its power from two overhead wires, in 1899 and again at the 1900 Paris Exhibition.

Experiments continued throughout Europe and in 1908 the Railless Electric Traction Company was formed here in England. There had to be two wires to provide both the feed and return electric current (trams used the running rails for the return). The first systems used a small trolley which ran on top of the two wires, and the two power cables then passed between the wires and dangled loosely

Two very early trolley buses on the outskirts of York. I suspect the one on the right has collected passengers from the broken down bus on the left which now bears the destination 'Depot'. (Transport for London – London Transport Museum Collection)

down to the bus roof. The bus thus dragged its trolley along behind and this gave the term 'trolley' to these vehicles. In Britain the use of two separate poles pressing up below the wires was preferred and later became standard for much of the world.

The first routes to use trolley buses were opened in Leeds and Bradford in 1911, followed by Rotherham and many other towns over the next few years. All these schemes replaced trams but many were abandoned after a fairly short time, sometimes due to the way the better acceleration tore up the road surface. Some were extensions of tram lines, like the Rotherham line to Maltby (which ran until 1954), but only two trolley bus schemes

A six-wheel Derby Transport trolley bus photographed in 1936 as part of a rush hour study to consider where road improvements could be best applied. Apart from more buses and a single lorry, it seems that bicycles make up the rush! (Derby Museum and Art Gallery))

The distinctive and ever popular London Transport red. (From the East Anglia Transport Museum)

The distinctive yellow of the Bournemouth fleet seen here in the tram sheds at the Black Country Museum. Just as with the trams and buses, each area had its own distinctive colour scheme.

were built where trams had never been, in Ramsbottom in Lancashire and Teesside. The manager of the Teesside system, a Mr J. Boothroyd Parker, took a different approach and instead of looking at the trolley bus as a trackless tram, in 1922 he modified a Tilling-Stevens petrol-electric bus to run either on its petrol engine or on the overhead trolley bus wires. Looking at the project as a variation of a bus rather than a tram altered the public's perception and many say this completely changed the future of the trolley bus.

Somewhat sporadically, trolley buses replaced trams in many towns. They were cleaner and quieter than the motor buses and they had the ability to run an alarming distance from the wires, giving versatility to stop near the kerb or to pass parked vehicles.

This last feature was attractive to many corporations who had long sections of single-track tramway which simply couldn't cope with the demand. The overhead wires already existed and only had to be changed to the two-wire system. The tram tracks were either simply covered over or lifted as scrap and the road rebuilt in a conventional manner. By the end of 1930, 34 tramway systems had changed to the motor bus whilst eleven chose trolley buses. There were also political pressures: the trolley bus ran on the locally generated electricity which used coal as its fuel, the motor bus used imported oil and this was a time of unemployment in the coal mines. Another pressure was that, in 1930, the Road Traffic Act took

Another Black Country Museum tram on duty giving rides; in the livery of the Birmingham Corporation.

much freedom away from motor bus operators but left the trams and trolley buses to choose their own routes and fares.

It was perhaps because there was no clear overwhelming advantage between the motor bus, the tram or the trolley bus that different cities chose different solutions.

In the 1930s a further 26 systems converted either completely or partially to the trolley bus, the biggest being London. Here conversion started in 1931 followed by other

A 1950-built six wheel Daimler trolley bus fitted with a body by Roe's. On display and giving rides at the Sandtoft Museum, this one is from Rotherham.

Showing just how far a trolley bus can move from the line of the overhead wires is this 1937-built South Shields bus with a Weymann body on a Karrier E4 chassis.

light traffic routes in 1933, trams still holding sway for heavy traffic central routes. In 1936, however, the LCC decided to convert all its tram routes to trolley buses except for a few miles that were judged best served by motor buses. In the ten years from 1930 to 1940, 82 of the 130 tram systems had closed. The process was held at bay by the Second World War but continued afterwards.

CHAPTER 7

The Romance Ends

A lonely electric tram stands surrounded by motor buses and cars. It's Bristol in 1939 and life is about to change forever. Within 25 years it will all be gone – steam trains, horses, trams and trolley buses. Only the motor bus will remain fighting for space among the ever-growing mass of cars.

The 1930s saw all the rivals trying to improve their systems – trams, motor buses and trolley buses. Tram development had all but finished by 1930 but they were now running some very smooth and comfortable machines. Many had air or magnetic track brakes whose ability to stop the tram smoothly and quickly meant higher speeds could be allowed. Strangely, the style changed very little despite strides being made in America and on the Continent. There were exceptions – for instance, in Liverpool, where the 1935 'Green Goddesses' arrived. Sunderland, Sheffield, Glasgow, Edinburgh, Blackpool and Leeds all continued to build new trams in the 1930s. The cost of maintaining the track was an ever-increasing problem, however, and nobody really believed that the trams

The Liverpool Corporation 'Green Goddess' tram showing what perhaps might have been.

would survive. Only the approaching war would hold back replacement, leaving some still running until 1952.

On the other hand, motor buses were just getting into their stride, with both single and double deck models looking modern and comfortable. The coach, basically just a well appointed single deck bus, was establishing itself as the medium and long distance vehicle of choice, as the railways knew all too well. Special buses had been made to cope with low railway bridges or ancient gates into medieval towns. These had the upstairs walkway lowered to protrude over the heads of the downstairs passengers, thus taking nearly 18 inches off the total

(left) Upstairs in a 'Low Bridge' bus with the lowered walkway and low headroom over the seats. And (right) the resultant bump in the roof above the downstairs seating.

Less busy routes and rural services were served by hardworking basic single deck buses. These London Transport GS buses are said to have inspired 'Bertie the Bus' known to many children.

This Bedford coach was typical of privately-run coaches used for excursions and contract work.

height. Being awkward to negotiate, they were not popular but they had almost the same seating capacity of a normal double deck bus and avoided the massive costs of lowering roads.

In 1930 Tom Barton fitted a Gardner marine diesel engine into one of his buses, showing good performance

and lower fuel consumption. The diesel engine had been around for many years but was not thought versatile enough for the stop-start life of a bus. In 1933 the Guy 'Arab' bus had a diesel engine fitted, to be followed by AEC and Leyland, all

More serious coach work needed larger capacity coaches with greater comfort.

As soon as the M1 reached Birmingham, Midland Red planned a service using high specification coaches. This one, new in 1965, worked on the motorway until 1974.

The Atlantean from Leyland with a Metro Cammell body was a workhorse of the 1960s and 70s, with concertina doors and a rear mounted engine. This one was in harness from 1960 to 1981, having covered 1¼ million miles!

of whom supplied the bus chassis. Nearly all buses and trams are built as a chassis complete with engine, wheels, etc., onto which is bolted the body, invariably made by another company. Further development saw the engine moved – sometimes behind the driver, sometimes under an admittedly high floor, each change designed to maximize the seating capacity. Leyland produced a small single deck bus called the 'Cub' which had a rear-mounted diesel engine. This arrangement was to become very popular in time on both single and double deck buses and coaches. The engines had also improved from the early units which had struggled to reach 20 hp but now were producing over 75 hp; six-wheeled, 66-seater double deck buses using these more powerful engines were introduced in 1927. Another improvement was the chassis, which was no longer a flat lorry type but was now shaped such that the bus floor was lower and carried a much improved suspension.

During the 1930s the road network continued to improve, smooth tar-macadam surfacing having become universal. The arrival of the Second World War naturally put everything on hold. Moving troops and materials took priority and public transport – the trains, trams, buses and trolley buses – struggled with a minimum of staffing and maintenance. After the war the country awoke to devastated transport systems, worn out and needing vast amounts of investment. Nothing that could not show itself to be economic would be allowed.

On the roads the versatile motor bus was obviously the way to go, able to use any route, to easily divert around major road repairs and using

a technology shared with the world of the commercial lorry. At the same time the austerity of the period seemed to generate a desire to disconnect from the past, resulting in frankly ghastly architecture with complete disregard for the style or atmosphere of our cities. Trains, trams and even trolley buses seemed of the past, almost Victorian. As always there were exceptions, particularly on the railways where all the companies were amalgamated under British Railways and a complete range of new steam engines put into production. Partly driven by our having plenty of coal, this decision seemed fairly logical in the 1950s but was to be alarmingly short lived.

I would like to briefly return to the oldest form of public transport that is still with us today, the taxi. Taxis – beginning as the hackney – had continued as horse-drawn vehicles of

The taximeter was originally mechanically driven like early speedometers in cars. The timing was by a hand-wound spring clock. (London Vintage Taxi Association)

A pair of 'Rational' taxis wait for fares outside the Savoy Theatre in 1905. (Transport for London – London Transport Museum Collection)

various sizes right through to the start of the 20th century when, for a brief three years, electric cars were tried. They had enjoyed, if that is the right term, regulation from as far back as 1636 when Charles I had limited the number of taxis in London to 50. In 1662 taxis had to be licensed and by 1833 both the vehicle and the driver had to be 'fit and proper'.

The term 'taxi' came in 1891 when Baron von Thurn und Taxis (Wihelm Bruhn) invented the 'taximeter', which measured the distance travelled and the time taken for each journey, the fares incidentally being laid down by Parliament. Prior to this, one simply bartered with the driver. Petrol engine vehicles took over the role with the French Unic cab, imported by Mann & Overton, becoming the most common. The relatively small number of vehicles needed always meant that their manufacture was a somewhat hit and miss affair, though some very well-known names appeared and disappeared over the years – American Fords, Vauxhall, Rover, Fiat, Austin, Humber and Wolseley, plus several French companies, all dabbled with taxis but had gone by 1914. The Scottish company W. Beardmore produced the first post-war (1919) taxi but in the 1930s the Austin name reappeared and become the most common make. The product underwent many changes of ownership with different sponsors and different engines until, in 1997, production of the then current version, the FX4, ended after more than 75,000 had been made.

(right) The French Unic taxi built in Paris and introduced in 1906, a year before taximeters became compulsory. (London Vintage Taxi Association)

An Austin 12/4 taxi from the mid 1930s. Note the fold-down cover over the rear seats. Taxis had been banned from Hyde Park for many years up to 1920 because of improper behaviour by the passengers. (London Vintage Taxi Association)

A more recognisable version from the 1950s. Taxis have never had to be painted in black even though after 1940 most were. (London Vintage Taxi Association)

CHAPTER 8

The Dust Settles

It is now 1963 and all the horses, trams and trolley buses have gone. Public transport is now represented by the motor bus and the railway. This was Nottingham's main bus station and the railway viaduct carried the ex-Great Central Line from London, which, alas, was closed within three years of this photo. (George L. Roberts)

The various horse-drawn vehicles had all faded in the wake of the railways and later the motor bus. By the end of the 1930s the future of the tram and trolley bus was also virtually sealed, though the war was to delay this until the 1950s and 1960s. The rural railway system had also succumbed to the motor bus, coach and lorry. The 1970s thus dawned to a much simpler public transport situation – taxis took care of local personal movements, the buses served mass movements within the cities and towns, and coaches and trains looked after the medium inter-city traffic. The railways would have liked to specialize in long-distance freight and passenger movements but were obliged to maintain the rarely profitable suburban networks without which most large cities would have simply seized up. The airplane settled into long-distance overland routes and its natural strength, the overseas journey.

Though each sector developed more modern-looking machines, nothing really changed until the 1990s when, pressed by sometimes desperate commuter overcrowding, we rediscovered the tram, a mode of transport which many Continental cities had never abandoned. The tram's fixed location was seen as a problem but it can also be a virtue. As a car driver or pedestrian, one knows exactly where the tram will go and it can pass through gaps that are just wide enough in a way that motor

The Midland Metro linking Birmingham and Wolverhampton. Most of the route uses an old GWR railway track bed with only a mile or so being true tramway.

The modern bus, ideal for medium and long journeys. Unlike the trains it still has to fight its way through traffic jams in the rush hour but it can go where people need it and not to just where the Victorian builders thought we might want to go.

vehicles could never do. In some ways it is like a bus-only-lane but one that other vehicles can use or cross when there are no trams around. In Britain most 'new' tram networks also make use of old railway tracks to move between city centres and the surrounding suburbs.

Today those railways that survived are busier than ever and, frankly, offer a much better service; coaches pound our motorways and buses still move masses in the towns. Even the delightful rural bus has recovered, usually subsidised and dependent on carrying schoolchildren from outlying villages, as well as the elderly non-car-owning population.

But, what of the future? I don't think anyone has ever correctly anticipated the direction public transport has taken in the past and the public's short memory will always prevent the virtues of earlier systems from being recognized. If the truth were told, nobody wants to use public transport now that private cars have become so much a part of our lives, so the future will probably depend on how convenient and comfortable public transport can be made and how overcrowded our roads and motorways become. Oh, yes, and how much it costs to park our cars!

Please remember many museums are staffed by volunteers and are not necessarily open every day, so before setting out check the websites for up-to-date information.

Amberley Museum, Amberley, nr Arundel, W. Sussex BN18 9LT
www.amberleymuseum.co.uk;
telephone: 01798 831370
Good selection of vehicles in ex-quarry site.

Aston Manor Road Transport Museum, 208-216 Witton Lane, Birmingham B6 6QE
www.amrtm.org; telephone: 0121 322 2298
Historic and classic vehicles housed in an old tram depot.

Birmingham & Midland Museum of Transport, Chapel Lane, Wythall, Worcs B47 6JX
www.bammot.org.uk; telephone: 01564 826471
Good selection of Midland buses.

Black Country Living Museum, Tipton Road, Dudley, West Midlands DY1 4SQ
www.bclm.co.uk; telephone: 0121 557 9643
Very varied museum which runs both a tram and trolleybus service.

British Commercial Vehicle Museum, King Street, Leyland, Lancs PR25 2LE
www.bcvm.org.uk; telephone: 01772 451011
Excellent museum covering many types of commercial transport.

Castle Point Transport Museum, Canvey Island, Essex SS8 7TD
www.castlepointtransportmuseum.co.uk; telephone: 01268 684272
Home to over 30 old and rare buses and coaches.

Cobham Bus Museum, Redhill Road, Cobham, Surrey KT11 1EF
www.lbpt.org; telephone: 01932 868665
Concentrates on open days when buses can be seen running.

Coventry Transport Museum, Millennium Place, Hales, Coventry CV1 1JD
www.transport-museum.com;
telephone: 024 7623 4270
Large museum with wide range of transport examples.

Crich Tramway Village, nr Matlock, Derbyshire DE4 5DP
www.tramway.co.uk; telephone: 01773 854321
Delightful recreated Edwardian street complete with trams giving rides and home to the National Tramway Museum.

East Anglia Transport Museum, Chapel Road, Carlton Colville, Lowestoft NR33 8BL
www.eatm.org.uk; telephone: 01502 518 459
A living museum where vehicles of yesteryear can be seen in action.

Ipswich Transport Museum, Old Trolleybus Depot, Cobham Road, Ipswich IP3 9JD
www.ipswichtransportmuseum.co.uk; telephone: 01473 715666
Collection of transport items devoted to Ipswich.

Isle of Wight Bus Museum, Newport Quay, Newport, Isle of Wight PO30 2EF
www.iowbusmuseum.org.uk; telephone: 01983 533352
An impressive display of vintage buses and coaches.

Keighley Bus Museum, Riverside Depot, Keighley, West Yorkshire BD21 4JU
www.kbmt.org.uk; telephone: 01282 413179
A charitable trust, the museum is run by volunteers so phone for opening times.

Lincolnshire Road Transport Museum, Whisby Road, North Hykeham, Lincoln LN6 3QT
www.lvvs.org.uk; telephone: 01522 689497
Collection of vintage buses, cars and commercial vehicles.

London Transport Museum, Covent Garden Piazza, London WC2E 7BB
www.ltmuseum.co.uk; telephone: 020 7379 6344
Lively museum with some very nice examples of London's transport.

Manchester Museum of Road Transport, Boyle Street, Cheetham Hill, Manchester M8 8UW
www.gmts.co.uk; telephone: 0161 205 2122
Friendly site with some nice examples.

Milestones Living History Museum, Leisure Park, Basingstoke RG22 6PG
www.milestones-museum.com; telephone: 0845 603 5635
Vintage vehicles in a realistic setting.

North West Museum of Transport, The Old Bus Depot, Hall Street, St Helens WA10 1DU
www.hallstreetdepot.info; telephone: 01744 451681
Vintage buses, British trolleybuses and classic cars.

Nottingham Transport Heritage Centre, Ruddington, NG11 6NX
www.nthc.co.uk; telephone: 01159 405705
Collection of historic buses and heritage railway.

Oxford Bus Museum, Main Road, Long Hanborough, Witney OX29 8LA
www.oxfordbusmuseum.org.uk; telephone: 01993 883617
Excellent bus museum with lots to see.

Sandtoft Trolleybus Museum, Belton Road, Sandtoft, Doncaster DN8 5SX
www.sandtoft.org.uk; telephone: 01724 711391
Largest trolleybus museum in Europe, normally only working on open days so always check.

South Yorkshire Transport Museum, Aldwarke, Rotherham, S65 3SH
www.sytm.co.uk; telephone: 0114 2553010
Restored trams and buses once in use in and around Sheffield.

ACKNOWLEDGEMENTS

I would like to record my thanks to the dozens of owners of restored vehicles who visit the many transport events for the simple pleasure of displaying their work to others. A special thanks must go to the many people at the various museum sites who answered my never-ending questions and queries and whose tireless restoration work provides many of the pictures in the book. Their enthusiasm is contagious and hopefully will inspire any reader who visits.